I0843104

Did you know that you can move to Canada without an employer-based visa? It's true! Using the Express Entry Federal Skilled Workers Program, you can immigrate to Canada if you have certain job skills and enough money to support yourself for a few months. This 11 page guide tells you everything you need to know to (1) determine if you qualify (2) and what steps to take to ensure a smooth and easy application process. Guaranteed to save you hours and hours of research! Time is money. Isn't it time that you move to Canada?

Self-sponsorship is a great immigration path if you
- Do NOT want your immigration status tied to a specific employer
- Do NOT intend to live in the Province of Quebec
- ARE interested in a path to citizenship (permanent residents are eligible for citizenship after 3 years)
- PREFER to search for employment after relocation
- WORK REMOTELY and would like to live in Canada
- ARE over the age of 35; younger people can apply too, but the Express Entry Federal Skilled Worker Program is one of the few pathways available to people 35 and older.

Table of Contents

The Express Entry Federal Skilled Worker Program (FSWP) provides an opportunity for individuals and accompanying family members to gain permanent residence in Canada and live any province or territory except for Quebec (which has a similar application process and requires proof of proficiency in French). The program is considered an economic class route to permanent residence. Applicants to the Express Entry FSWP **must** (1) have certain skills (defined by the National Occupation Classification, NOC) and (2) be sponsored by an employer or self-sponsor. **This guide focuses exclusively on self-sponsorship.**

Self-sponsorship means that if you can prove sufficient cash funds to sustain yourself and any accompanying family members you do **NOT** need to secure employment before applying for permanent residency. The amount of money needed can be found HERE. It ranges from $12,300 CAD for a single adult (and increases an additional $3,000 to $3,300 CAD per family member based on total family size).

You can read more about the NOC, eligible skills level (0, A, and B) and how to determine your **NOC code(s)** HERE.

Self-sponsorship is a great immigration path if you meet the NOC and financial guidelines and...

- Do NOT want your immigration status tied to a specific employer
- Do NOT intend to live in the Province of Quebec

- ARE interested in a path to citizenship
- PREFER to search for employment after relocation; or
- WORK REMOTELY and would like to live in Canada
- SECURE rights and obligations in Canada (health care, public education, **Canada Child Benefit**, file taxes, etc.)
- ARE 35 years old or older; younger people can apply too, but the FSWP is one of only a few available to people 35 and older

Permanent residence is generally granted for 5 years and is renewable. If you reside within Canada for at least 3 years (or 1095 days) within the 5-year period, you are then eligible to apply for Canadian Citizenship once you have met 1095 days.

The FSWP is a point based immigration program. You receive points for your age, marital status, education, etc. The highest score possible is 1200. Detailed information about the Comprehensive Ranking System (CRS) **HERE**.

Visit this **LINK** to see how many people have applied and the CRS score of the lowest scoring candidate that was invited to apply for residence. (Note: for the June 25, 2018 round the lowest CRS score invited to apply was 442).

Check your eligibility for the program **HERE**.

Citizenship and Immigration provides and brief outline of the **application process**.

As a Permanent Resident, you can...
Apply for a Social Insurance Number
Access the Canadian health care system
Apply for and receive the Canada Child Benefit
Enroll your children in free public school
Open a bank account
Establish credit history in Canada
Work for a Canadian organizations or businesses
Start your own Canadian organization or business
Become eligible for paid **pregnancy leave** (up to 15 weeks) and/or **parental leave** (up to 35 weeks after birth or adoption)

*** To successfully enter the Candidate pool, you must first create a <u>CIC Account</u>. If you have not received **BOTH** your language exam scores and your Educational Credential Assessment (ECA), your application will be marked ineligible.

<u>Begin the ECA and Police Certificate report immediately</u>. The Police Certificate will be discussed in the next section, *Invitation to Apply*. The ECA will likely be the most time-consuming part of the process. Depending on which approved credentialing agency you choose the process can take up to 6 months. The actual review of your credentials doesn't take that long, it's waiting in line/queue that takes so long. Learn more <u>HERE</u>.

Call or E-mail each credentialing agency to get a wait time estimate. Also, make sure you have copies of each diploma you earned (request reprints from your university if needed).

When mailing copies of your diplomas and other ECA related paperwork, send in a single envelope using a 1-3 day expedited delivery service such as FedEx International First, FedEx International Priority.

If you are within the United States, Global Express Guaranteed is a 1-3 day service you can purchase at any United States Post Service (USPS) office (service from a main postal branch will typically be completed within 1 business day, delivery from a smaller post offices take 3 days). ***Note:***

you will need to include customs forms with the documents, so its best/simplest to visit a USPS or FedEx location.

You will need to complete the **International English Language Testing System's (IELTS) General Training Test**. There are over 1,100 IELTS testing sites in over 140 countries. Use this LINK to find your nearest testing center. You may need to travel and secure overnight accommodations to take the exam. Results valid for 12 months.

Once this application is submitted....
- Your profile will remain active for 12 months. If you do not receive an invitation to apply for permanent residency within the next 12 months, you will need to resubmit your application.
- You may receive notice that a province is interested in nominating you through the Provincial Nominee Program (PNP). Although this will give you an additional 600 points in the CRS, it costs roughly $1000 CAD and has a separate application process. Check if your total CRS score exceed the lowest score invited to apply before choosing the PNP. Note: the PNP process is not covered in this guide.

Once you have completed the initial phase and entered the candidate pool, you may receive an invitation to apply at any time. The invitation will be posted via notification within your CIC Account. New ITAs are typically sent twice per month, dates vary. Once you receive the ITA you have 90 days in which to submit all your documents via the CIC Account and pay your application fees. These documents will be uploaded to your application. Access to a scanner, or an app such as TinyScanner (download from Google Play or iTunes), or websites such as https://www.pdfmerge.com/ will be necessary.

Police Certificate(s)

You must provide a Police Certificate for EVERY country that you have lived in or visited for 6 months or more since the age of 18 (accumulated in a single visit or multiple visits over time). You and any family member who is over 18 will need to provide police certificates. To learn how to obtain police certificates visit this SITE.

Medical Exam(s)

Medical exams are only valid for 6 months and must be completed with a CIC approved panel physician. To learn more about medical exams and locate your nearest provider visit this SITE. You and your family members may need to travel and secure overnight accommodations to complete your medical exam. NOTE: Prices of medical exam varies by provider, be sure to call and compare prices.

Marriage & Name Change Documents

You will need to upload copies of these documents.

Marriage Certificate or Divorce, Name Change, & Child Custody Documents

You will need to upload copies of these documents
Any non-custodial parents will need to complete and
notarize a IMM 5604 form.

Birth Certificate(s)

You will need to upload copies of these documents.

Passport(s)

You will need to copy the photo and signature page of your
passport **AND** each page that contains a visa or entry/exit
stamp.

Digital Photo(s)

These photos must meet Immigration, Refugees, and
Citizenship Canada (IRCC) STANDARDS. Note: These
standards are extremely strict. Depending on the quality of
photographers in your area, you may need to visit a
professional photography studio- the picture MUST NOT
have any shadows or glare and MUST be on a WHITE
background. NOTE: The size of the photo must be: "50 mm x
70 mm (2 inches wide x 2 3/4 inches long) and sized so the
height of the face measures between 31 mm and 36 mm (1
1/4 inches and 1 7/16 inches) from chin to crown of head
(natural top of head)". This is not very important for the ITA
stage but is critical in the final Confirmation of Permanent
Residency Stage. The size and face proportions are larger

than US Passport Photos and many other countries. You must ask the photographer for their original jpeg or jpg files. You can submit these digital files for this step, and you can use the digital files to print your photos for the final phase (Confirmation of Permanent Residence).

A Complete list of mandatory documents can be found HERE.
Note: For EACH document that is in a language other than English or French, you must provide the (1) the original document (2) a version translated by a certified translator, and (3) an affidavit from the person who completed the translation(s).

Update your application
If you need to update your address, provide updates in your financial or marital status, or ask questions about your application you can do so online line via this LINK. Select "Tell us more", "yes", "no", and "Go to Web form".

When your application is nearly approved, you will receive an e-mail message at the account associated with your CIC Account profile. The title of the message is, "Ready for Visa / Prêt pour Visa". Read this message **very carefully** to determine which documents and forms need to be mailed via post **based on your country of citizenship**.

NOTE: When mailing your documents and photos send them in a single envelope using a 1-3 day expedited deliver service such as FedEx International First, FedEx International Priority. If you are within the United States, Global Express Guaranteed is a 1-3 day service you can purchase at any United States Post Service (USPS) office (service from a main postal branch will typically be completed within 1 business day, delivery from a smaller post offices takes 3 days). Note: you will need to include customs forms with the documents, so its best/simplest to visit a USPS or FedEx location.

PHOTOS

The most important thing in this step is to make sure your photos are printed according to IRCC STANDARDS. If you receive your confirmation of Permanent Residence within 30 days, you can use the same photo from the ITA but be sure to write the required information on the back of the photo(s) as instructed in the IRCC Standards.

There are 2 recommended online services for printing photos...

<u>MyPassportPhotos.com</u>
You can have the photos professionally reviewed/edited, sized according to IRCC Standards, and pick up next day at any Walmart, Walgreens, Target, or CVS. Or receive via mail delivery or instant digital download.
<u>NOTE</u>: when having photos printed at Walmart, Walgreens, Target, or CVS, the photos will include lines to show you where to cut.

<u>PassportPhotoNow.com</u>
You can have the photos professionally reviewed/edited, sized according to IRCC Standards, printed and mailed to you (next day shipping available), a CD and or/digital file download.

RETURN SHIPPING LABEL

The "Ready for Visa / Prêt pour Visa" email for **US residents** states a, "**Self-Addressed** pre-paid envelope should be arranged with a courier **that delivers between Canada and the U.S.A.**" This can be most conveniently arranged by via FedEx online using the instructions below. If you are **not** in Canada or the United States, follow the instruction in your email closely and do not hesitate to contact CIC as instructed in the e-mail you received. **They are very responsive, often answering within a single business day.**

To purchase a FedEx online shipping label please follow the instructions below.

- You will need to create a FEDEX account to complete your online purchase if you do not already have one.
- If you need help call FedEx at <u>1-800-463-3339</u>.

(1) **CONTROL & CLICK ON THIS** <u>LINK</u>

(2) **FILL IN THE SHIP "FROM"** address section with the CPC-Ottawa mailing address as below:
<u>First Name</u>: CPC-Ottawa | CTD-Ottawa
<u>Last Name</u>: PR-TR PRINTING | IMPRESSION RP-RT
<u>Email</u>: **(Your** email address)
<u>Street Number</u>: 365
<u>Street Name</u>: Laurier Ave
<u>Direction</u>: West
<u>City</u>: Ottawa
<u>Province</u>: Ontario
<u>Postal Code</u>: K1A 1L1

(3) **FILL IN THE SHIP "TO"** address section with your mailing address details

(4) **DESCRIBE ITEM**: Weight (kg): 0.200kg, Length (cm): 24 Width: 16 Height: 1

(5) **SELECT YOUR SERVICE** (Priority, Overnight, Saturday Delivery, etc.)

(6) **FOR PICK-UP** select Item #3 – pre-arranged pickup

(7) **REVIEW** all mailing details and pay online

VERY IMPORTANT TO FOLLOW THESE INSTRUCTIONS
When you receive the e-mail confirmation from FedEx - do not print out the label - open the shipping label and

<u>SAVE</u> the label as an electronic version (PDF file) on the desktop of your computer, <u>THEN PRINT.</u>

(8) PRINT THE PDF FILE LABEL and mail with package.

Once CIC has processed the photos and requested information you will receive your confirmation of permanent residence (COPR) document(s). You officially become a Canadian Permanent resident AFTER you cross a Canadian border (via air, rail, or bus) and present your COPR documents to an immigration officer.

YOU MUST ENTER CANADA BY THE EXPIRATION DATE INDICATED ON YOUR COPR DOCUMENT(S).

Typically, the COPR expires on the 1 year anniversary of your medical exam or 6 months before your passport expires- whichever comes first. If you are immigrating as a family, be sure to **REVIEW EACH COPR – there may be different dates of expiration.**

You will receive your permanent resident cards via post in roughly 60 days at the mailing address you provided to the immigration officer when you crossed the border.

OVERVIEW

Self-Sponsorship proof of funds:
http://www.cic.gc.ca/english/immigrate/skilled/funds.asp

National Occupation Classification Information:
https://www.canada.ca/en/immigration-refugees-citizenship/services/immigrate-canada/express-entry/become-candidate/eligibility/find-national-occupation-code.html

Canada Child Benefit:
https://www.canada.ca/en/revenue-agency/services/child-family-benefits/canada-child-benefit-overview.html

Comprehensive Ranking System:
https://www.canada.ca/en/immigration-refugees-citizenship/services/immigrate-canada/express-entry/become-candidate/criteria-comprehensive-ranking-system/grid.html

Current CRS Score Cut Off:
https://www.canada.ca/en/immigration-refugees-citizenship/services/immigrate-canada/express-entry/become-candidate/rounds-invitations.html

Express Entry Federal Skilled Worker Eligibility Checker:
https://www.canada.ca/en/immigration-refugees-citizenship/services/come-canada-tool.html

CIC Overview of Express Entry Federal Skilled Worker Program: https://www.canada.ca/en/immigration-refugees-citizenship/services/immigrate-canada/express-entry/apply-permanent-residence.html

ENTER THE CANDIDATE POOL

Create your CIC Account:
https://www.canada.ca/en/immigration-refugees-citizenship/services/application/account.html

Educational Credentialing Assessment:
https://www.canada.ca/en/immigration-refugees-citizenship/services/immigrate-canada/express-entry/become-candidate/eligibility/education-assessed.html

International English Language Testing System's (IELTS) General Training Test: https://www.ielts.org/book-a-test/find-a-test-location

INVITATION TO APPLY

TinyScaner:
https://play.google.com/store/apps/details?id=com.appxy.tinyscanner&hl=en
https://itunes.apple.com/us/app/tiny-scanner-pdf-scanner-to-scan-document-receipt-fax/id595563753?mt=8

PDF Merge:
https://www.pdfmerge.com/

Police Certificates:
https://www.canada.ca/en/immigration-refugees-citizenship/services/application/medical-police/police-certificates/how.html

Medical Exams:
https://www.canada.ca/en/immigration-refugees-citizenship/services/application/medical-police/police-certificates/how.html

Child Custody Form:
https://www.canada.ca/content/dam/ircc/migration/ircc/english/pdf/kits/forms/imm5604e.pdf

(IRCC) Photo Specification:
http://www.cic.gc.ca/EnGLIsh/information/applications/guides/pdf/5445EB-e.pdf

Additional Requirements:
https://www.canada.ca/en/immigration-refugees-citizenship/corporate/publications-manuals/operational-bulletins-manuals/permanent-residence/express-entry/applications-received-on-after-january-1-2016-completeness-check.html

Update your submitted application or ask questions:
http://www.cic.gc.ca/english/contacts/web-form.asp

Photo Printing for Confirmation of Permanent Residence Documents:
MyPassportPhotos.com
PassportPhotoNow.com

CONFIRMATION OF PERMANENT RESIDENCE

FedEx Self-Addressed Shipping Label:
https://www.fedex.com/lite/lite-ship.html?locale=en_ca&cntry_code=ca_english%23address#address

NOTES

NOTES

NOTES

NOTES

NOTES

NOTES

www.ingramcontent.com/pod-product-compliance
Lightning Source LLC
Chambersburg PA
CBHW061329250726
48657CB00003B/1099